MW01231664

# By Blanshard & Blanshard

*'Make Love Last. Fly Me To The Moon And Back.'*

*'Make Love Last (forever and a day) Dance Me To The Stars.'*

*'Memoir Of Love And Art , Honey In The Blood.'*

# HONEY IN
# THE BLOOD

# HONEY IN THE BLOOD

## Memoir Of Love And Art.

*Blanshard & Blanshard*

# Contents

# Review for *Honey in the Blood* by Rob Mars

The most poetic, beautiful memoir I have ever read *****

It is always fascinating to read a love story. *The more it is, if it spans 40 years of deep love, sexual desire, sensuality and creative art.* This poetic narrative illuminates the images and colors of the life with an artist by creating paintings with words. The words flow as the paint brush moves on the canvas and all of a sudden, figures, gestures and subject emerge from the colored points and lines. And when you read further, deeper, and let the lines of the narrative blur, they reveal behind themselves the whole world of two, a love for life and a life for love.

Susan Blanshard lets us peek into her amazingly rich life, in feelings and sensuality. She also masterly helps us approach the way an artist creates his masterpieces. She does not achieve this by photographs or description of techniques: She simply draws us in through her poetry. Her use of words and sentences create feeling s in us the same way we could see-read pictures of the artist, drink - absorb the colors and create our own reflections of the images in our own mind, together with feelings that emanate from them depending on our own experiences.

There are more quotes I loved in this book but probably the most expressive is the last sentence: "*A personal life deeply lived, expands into truths beyond itself and provides our own answers to the question of a man and a woman's love.*"

Highly recommended for all looking for these answers - and who isn't?

# Forward for *Honey in the Blood*
## by Raymond Keen

"Lovers don't finally meet somewhere. They're in each other all along."

- Rumi -

"Why is love beyond all measure of other human possibilities so rich and such a sweet burden for the one who has been struck by it? Because we change ourselves into that which we love, and yet remain ourselves. . . . That the presence of the other breaks into our own life -- this is what no feeling can fully encompass. Human fate gives itself to human fate, and it is the task of pure love to keep this self-surrender as vital as on the first day."

- Martin Heidegger -

What is human love? There is no clear or final answer. Or, rather, there are as many answers as there are persons who are or have ever been in love. There is spiritual love *(Agápe)*, love for family and friends *(Philia),* and sensual-romantic-sexual love *(Éros).*

In *Honey in the Blood*, Susan and Bruce Blanshard are writing about all of these kinds of love in describing their 40-year relationship. It is not so much writing "about," as it is *making present* the reality of this all-encompassing love bond shared by them. It is a man-woman relationship of the mind, heart and soul --- and it is so profound a description of this love that we are actually able to experience how this woman enters the existence of this man, and how this man enters the existence of this woman, and how both are transformed forever.

Yes, this love is sensual and sexual. Yet it is also spiritual in the deepest sense. The language to describe this living, breathing, pulsing love is poetry, and one can say with calm assurance that

*Honey in the Blood* is sustained prose poetry.

One may or may not have a better understanding of love-in-general after reading this book. But one *will* have a deep understanding of an utterly unique love between two human beings that has been sustained in intensity as lovers, friends, marriage partners, soulmates and collaborators in art for 40 years.

I could not have imagined such a relationship as possible. Yet *Honey in the Blood* makes this impossibly beautiful relationship utterly real, as it resonates in prose poetry with language like this:

> You teach me how to shake rules from my blood. You show me the old world, nomad, gypsy, raider, sailor; to live without apologies. To be a woman at the place of rocks. How the beach is our survival; it gives us food and the warm sun that will not wear out. A place we find that shines and burnishes us, and unlike the city, does not tarnish us.

Poet and painter become not so much close to each other as *they become each other,* and as they become mirrors for each other. As they begin to exist in a shared reality, poet Susan describes her love in a painterly fashion, and painter Bruce describes his love for Susan in simple, exquisite prose. Susan writes to Bruce:

> Your river runs through my veins.

Susan has now been transformed through her love *for* a painter into herself a *painter with words*:

> We swim. The light from the sun filters through the surface. A ribbon of sapphires. Not solid gems but tiny particles crushed as if they were ultramarine blue cerulean ground by a great pestle: Prussian blue to cobalt with tinctures of indigo and shades of lapis, it is like swimming into all the beach glass of civilization sparkling before us. I see the same blue in your eyes. The water holds us like a secret.

Bruce answers with the pure elegance of simple truth:

You are so beautiful.

This is a most unusual and most rare memoir of love presented by two artists living, working and raising two children together: Two hearts, two minds, two souls as one - a poet and a painter seeing and writing and loving through and for the other.

This is a book of memories that began 40 years ago when Susan was 17 and Bruce was 22. These memories are alive today in these two lovers, and we are very blessed to be able to share in this miracle of living love by reading *Honey in the Blood.*

Raymond Keen
Author of *Love Poems for Cannibals*
January 2013

# Honey In The Blood

I will say our secret...
and what secrets are left remain in my wrist pulse
when I die,
stay in the bones of my spine?

Through my life lover,
I am left with traces of you,
fragments felt in everything I touch.

I entered your room without knocking as
if I walked into a room that felt like my own.
I can't say precisely what I came for.
I fell into your life like an angel,
an angel with strings
I fell through the Genesis hedge and topiary fig
into your walled garden.
I stayed quietly  falling in love
with the man I found there
until I forgot how to leave.

Before this moment, we were together
before stars were diamonds
chipped from a reef of sky
I wore your ring.
And I carried our child on my hip
your honey in my blood.

*Susan Blanshard 2004*

*(I think our lives were divinely turned inside out.*
*And a silk hand wrapped us up in each other)*

What lies ahead is not so much a story of us, but the river between us. At times the stillness of a meditation pool clear blue and you see right through. Other times, the reflections are my own, muddy and disturbed. Among them a time, cold as winter, the entire surface of the world we knew iced over. And impenetrable.

Life evolves. Because of chance meetings. Because of synchronicity and happenstance. We go to places for a reason. Perhaps we came to exist together because of the territorial layout of the city we met in. The capital city with its plethora of tunnels, cable cars, train tracks and overhead trolleybus cables. A city where giant plates of the earth suddenly slip out of sync. Our intimacy like a history, the dissipation back into physical is deeply geological. Our personal habits are more predictable than earthquakes. We go some place for a reason.

Whether you are born in the city or not, one city is an echo of another. You would think there was some scarcity of space in a city or that it was just a matter of time before we would finally meet each other.

A month before we met, we 'pre-met' without realizing this. If I observed you as a film extra, I see you pouring red wine. You may look at me when you hand me the glass, but I take no notice of your eyes. In another pre-meeting scene, I see you through a glass door. The proximity of you to the closeness of others. And the logic of speech. Your hands as they remain open, emanate, like a saint radiating, a halo or a crown.

Some magnetism happens. People surround you and your smile.

There are clues to the significance of what I observe. The future has its secret agenda. At no point can you foretell or figure out the plan of fate.

Some people resort to a stranger inking their palms, or scattering fortune cards or reading tea leaves. Whatever the artifacts of cards or dark leaves tell you, this reliance to predict and sooth-say has the opposite effect. When I want change in my life, the fortune-telling cards demonize hard times rather than bring the divine to intervene and bring forth grace and a helping of good luck. The horseman, swords and daggers create a puzzle. It seems no one tosses coins heads up in this life. I bring good fortune on myself as long as I can follow my passions. I must allow love, more than fortune to find itself.

Picasso said once: that as soon as an artist hangs a work of art, it no longer belongs to the artist. So art becomes an acquisition. People stare at what they have acquired, knowing that it has no place in their own soul.

You keep things from un-belonging to you by holding on to them. Looking at your paintings, I detect my own physical likeness, if not of me, then what you take from me. Or rather, what I give you.

As for my writing let me explain. I should explain that of the Muses, next to painting, writing is the most carnal. Discovering the blueprint of us - people would perhaps see that you and I have an obsession for the unmade bed, the anatomy of form, the bed which holds the infinity of contact with a lovers body, a sensation of all human desire that the body contains.

The first draft of 'Memoir Of Love And Art' was written when I suffered a severe bout of acute pneumonia. I take the suffocating heat in the tropics badly; breathing in the unmitigated toxin emitting from green spores and black mould still worse. Mould against the architraves and columns  projects to a jungle-like wall of wretchedly damp proportions. Rain from the balcony seeps under the wooden floorboards, mosquito reproduce in the dark, tiny larvae first hatching, then whining inside the mosquito netting.

I am one of those people who prefer to make choices. But in the moment of illness, the sense of place, of time; the heat, mould and mosquitoes are as abstract as watching a gecko inside the balloon of a red silk lampshade - it has no choice but to be there - it remains as trapped as you are.

I was told I might die. The doctor sending a letter to the embassy; the embassy contacting the foreign affairs department to red stamp my exit visa. A delay of six weeks.

We all harbor a fear of dying and a dead-end. That's why I hurried the ending. But the thing is I didn't die. As I write this now. I was surprised that even after a blind fortune-teller told me that I would die within a month, the amalgam of black and the afterlife never happened. I was amazed to wake up and see that although my face was pale, my body had not been absorbed into the ever after. There are better ways to die, I am sure. And I learned that one should never rush an earthly conclusion.

I have been returning to beginnings, with the frequency of a recurring dream. Yet there is a vague sense of illegibility of day-dreaming. Memory trains your eye inwards; you find the furnishings have replaced what existed before; the bed made up more elaborate. Even the lime washed walls appear as serious faced cherubs and angels carved in the splendor of plaster.

So here I am a decade later rewriting the manuscript but not the ending - in short, I can't write something that has not happened. Even then I can't. So in the honesty of truth - I will never know how life goes until I get to my last breath. If the last breath is impossible to express then one must focus on the starting point.

*(As a beginning, I think I shall start here)*


Forty years ago, Bluff oysters were two
dollars a dozen and

I was seventeen.

To dispel the vague sense of illegality,
counting the fingers like months on one hand
here, four months until September. I turned eigh-
teen.

You, my lover were twenty-two.

The backdrop for the first time we meet
was a room with a vast window, each pane the

color of church glass, the red and blue of saints; the rubies and sapphires of glass chipped off by the afternoon sun. The house you entered on a May afternoon was quiet. I was the only one there, asleep.

I woke to hear the sound of you, of the caddy spoon digging black tea leaves. It was a time of steam rising and the clicking of the power switch. Of scrutinizing the face of a sleeping girl, and I heard you do all this.

I believe making tea is high on the list of introductions for every stranger and that I had in mind the exact moment to open my eyes and the equally exact sound of your voice as you spoke to me for the first time. Tea was the beginning of us, if I had thought to turn your cup over; I would have seen my face in the wet tea-leaves.

It was a warm afternoon, and before my heart registered anything, I was taken by this feeling of being alone in the room with you; my eyes were filled with what has always been their synonym, the blue of your shirt. For some people it is the blue of the sky, for others the blue of the water or lilacs. I recognized certain elements in the blue of your shirt.

This attraction towards that blue could have been attributed to a childhood sitting in church on Sunday, with the sunlight pouring through the blue robes of the Saints. As for studying Angels, I had to imagine growing wings in order to catch the angelic. Yet the source of my attraction to you, I felt lay elsewhere, beyond the blue of saints, beyond the imprint of childhood, beyond the confines of biology, beyond one's own genetic make-up; somewhere in one's stores of impressions that began in the realms of the beginning of time.

Blue is an infinite color, of horizons that disappear as soon as you step off the water, blue is a road for returning souls as they walk across the river. Blue is the color of beginning. The eclipse of dreaming, the color of our baby's eyes.

Do we come full circle and now revert to what is between us. We return complete. Find a way back to each other. Getting back more and more of each other until you stand in the doorway looking into the room and instead of you, I am looking at us through all time, through the dark cage of my eye lashes I see you again. I can find my way into love only through feeling, because I have no control over what happens.

My experience of a man existed in abstract, a look, a note, but then you smiled and kissed me, you made my face hot. I knew where this was going. It felt like I had finally found you, in some insignificant place on the city map. Some pre-ordained meeting point - after perhaps life times of being apart.

Sleeping in the afternoon, if I had left before you arrived, I might have walked in another direction, or stepped on to a city bus. And even if I was passing you by, another lone figure walking on the street; or looked in another direction, I would have missed you, if you had opened another door. Yet, you didn't.

You begin by explaining that you are going

back to your studio, and perhaps I would like to walk with you. I like the sound of your voice. It is more formal than the invitation. I was thinking how to tell you that I can not stay. That it is late in the day and too early in my life for anything repeated and permanent. I should go, but do not find myself speaking those words. There is a power in your asking. A politeness and you don't wait for an answer. And the feeling so exquisite and tender, beyond all refusal.

Opening a door and entering where dreams cross over dream-crossed space. I can think how this relationship will end, the gradual subtraction, but when you speak, I skip the option and look into your eyes.


We walk through the park. We ignore the out-of-bounds, stroll across perfect green grass; blue in the sky caught momentarily in black and the coliseum of spectator seats empty. Suddenly everything is wet in a heavy downpour. There is something primordial about running through rain, especially if you get soaking wet.

Rain makes you more alert than you were before. When you run through rain together you sense a mutual danger, and you keep moving together in the same direction, you lose direction momentarily; the need to arrive becomes heightened. In the psychology of rain we sense each other more. We move in closer, moving in the same direction; in the ten minutes in the rain with you, I knew that our lives had merged closer.

We arrive at the Victorian villa east of the central city. The hallway suffused with the aroma of roasted coffee and the ubiquitous odor of rain.

That's how I find myself for the first time in your studio. As it turns out, there is one bathroom with six shower stalls and a separate bathroom room with a claw foot bath. There is something inspirational about the amount of faucets. "This house was once a brothel," you said.

I remember every intimate detail of what happened in that bedroom. What went on behind the door. Undressing down, until I was standing naked. Yes I wanted you. So I did the only thing I thought I could do with my mouth. I kissed you. I kissed lips that formed those beautiful words, every inch of your mouth with my tongue, to find a secret cove where your voice lay hidden.

Your face has a look of infinity, the very look deep and inviting, seeps into me, blood and flesh. We are like a floating ship surrounded by water, perpetual oceanography; everything becomes wet with it. We are two fish swimming through a sunken treasure ship. Our mouths fill with jewels, we can no longer breathe.

And so, that afternoon, the first kiss I gave you was enough to reach you, irresistible enough to take your heart and disturb its delicate secrets, as its rhythm echoed mine, deep ties of desire, so tight and delicate they break without us noticing.

My senses are always pulled towards you, as if you had studied the most seducing ways, without appearing to have studied them at all. Waiting for pleasures without seeking them. The unmade bed, an image of intimacy I return to. If I described heaven, you would be my astronomer.

The first room we make love in. A dark canvas bed painted in enormous flowers and tiny acorns and cherubs with unfathomable blue eyes, and painted ribbon scrolls - most likely gold. The overall feelings renaissance and mythological and in the distance, the sound of Mozart violin refrain, playing loudly, a pulse, as if the composer understood each physical movement. Between those movements, as my body presses against you. It is you making love to a part of my poetry.

I had already dreamed of having a place in a man's life, and now I find you. I wake up in your bed at the end of solitude, (this in my book of memory, will be interwoven) wild flower tea and wheat toast. I want to love you into words before the shadows of the future slip past us, to love you when we know each other, simply as lovers and dreamers, for loving you is what I want to discover, masculine smell on a throat (musk and leather) and one summer will remember us as color (honey and bronze).

The air in your room diffuses with freesias: the flowers, (double red blooms, amorously intermingled), arranged by instinct, perfumed for pleasure. There is a flower preserved for a long time in the room of memory. Here the flowers never lose perfume, the light through the window never fades, a glass vase on the sill, always full. With a faraway sound of rain falling outside the room. And a sound of murmuring, inviting that soft sadness which is the beginning of pleasure.

You walked over to the bed and sat close to me, kissing me on the lips - the meaning of love and sex and trouble, this secret vow, repeated thousands of times, more than first moment as if I hear you as your voice whispers, here we are, we are in this life together. I let you undress me and paint what you want. I did not interrupt you except to imprint more kisses. For you caught my eyes, like fire on a hill... maybe seen, as I see myself, the heat I find, one look from you and all my body burning. A few leaves jangling with tiny rust holes. Burning wild grasses and wild-flower brushed on the walls and you in this room. I have a match. No lighter.

Any moment triggers an image, and emotion repeats itself. For it is said, this bond and place, carries the weight of desire, one man and woman stealing all the desire of the world, if you wrapped a blindfold over my eyes, tapped the velvet bones with your hammer, there are enough moments inside me, to take over my body, for me to detect your fingers (trailing dreams) over my skin. So much of you will become part of me. Lover. You know this.

Folded, cut or torn; paper has memory and these words, intercepted in that moment, are yours. I am  chronicler of my own secrets. My words turning slowly on their own journey, some traveling backwards, some leading forwards to other things. Words can pull down the bloody moon; turn back the sun, make rivers flow upstream. Doors are no match for the binding; toughest locks can be opened by what is inside a book.

These pages are my footprints on the grass. I am absorbing all the moisture with my bare feet. I am taking responsibility for the dew there. I am posing naked on your mattress in a disused brothel, these evenings in the street- light room. Rethinking all the secrets that pull you into me, I am turning the page on my feelings about you, and me, and that receptive repeated intimacy. White sheets strewn with roses. A garden of scent at the edge of earthiness. Some of the fragments you know: touch, color. I am carving your name in the wind. The bed... it makes a noise... who will hear us!

If anyone could see into the room, the sepia and melon-skin walls visible when the windows are open: but if you look through the windows in order to see us kiss, you see moving shapes instead. The mattress shaping itself to curves, we press into it. So I slept with you there for six to seven months, until the winter when the light fell behind the mountain at four-thirty in the afternoon and the nights lasted fourteen hours.

I lie beside you and listen to each breath folding in and out of your lungs, a heart beating, repeating perfectly, caged by bones, whole life repetitions in circadian and primordial rhythm. Traversed by your body span, part muscle, part sinew. Strong steel of a man in the night. Like iron ore vice, hold me tight. Into the pulse, the moving and breathing, subtle like a shape of forged or softly welded parts. I want to be filled with you, sinew, muscle, bone; nothing to break the feeling of you.

You paint a beautiful geometry, of dream and surrender. You paint hair tousled and long. My hands as I push my hair away from my eyes. A sense of movement, the tension of colliding forces. Bringing to mind the myth of Pygmalion and Galatea, breathing life and an unexpected reciprocity on the lips when you kiss me.

The ceiling and walls of the room covered with wallpaper, of ghost palms and leaves: in the midst is a bed with white linen and pillows, a hothouse of white petals, ribbons and lace, as if it grows against wall.

I trace the curve of your eyes while you dream, what becomes of us while we sleep. The unnumbered kisses get lost in a crowd of warm kisses on warm lips and eyelids of eyes that swim in liquid dream, you pass your hands over my skin like genesis of rays over the whole earth, and your lips for some time remain, as if impossible to move away from you. I believe in the wedding of it. Your tongue in my mouth, I love your way of kissing. Imprint of your lips. You, who kiss like fire, summon my soul back. An untranslatable feeling in my mouth.

And I love you as you drift over my body and fill my mind like incense. I feel as if some fragrance spills over me. So the room where we first made love in keeps returning. The long, slow afternoons, with the moments of bright or fading light casting shadows on walls and ceiling, dividing my thoughts between what was and now is. These thoughts slip out easily, like my arms from my linen shirt, when I undress in front of you.

I see your jawbone, fixed like a slant of air. When you see me watching you, your smile breaks into an arc of love. Your smile is familiar to me. Then you smile again but it is the weight of your hand pressed in the small of my back that arouses me. As close as getting to know the secret feel of you, I no longer need to dream it.

It feels like a red-hot fire shut up inside a bone. Where nothing can contain it and only a flow can cool it. I feel as if I am waking from a dream. Into the arms of you who woke my sleeping body. One million years may have past before this moment. Then I find you again and every instinct breaks into life.

Your kiss, the scarcely perceptible salt in a

mouth. Your kiss on my lips carried by physical incantation, every kiss held, every release, unreal. Blindfolded destiny is complete seduction. I only know this secret  sacrament between us. And tomorrow, who knows if reminiscent winds will blow the air and our voices back together. I will always find you; the wind blowing through our infinite existence pushes our souls together.

I want to feel your body warmth from a distance. I want to be found by you, as the one traveled. All the doorways lead to cities of memory. Can I step over... move the sliding door? As I quietly found the key once and unlocked the door once, move deeper into the room, I know the room, all of our chambers, thinking of the dwelling, light in each archway. These nocturnal imaginings pressed against my skin. In which my skin registers shadow as a degree of black.

Could you paint my body as I give myself to you? Remembering the shift of the shadow. "I have never known a woman who feels like this," you said.  Then I watch you open your eyes and you look beyond my face. You look as if you have seen me, not just through a cage of dark eyelashes but further on, through veils of time. "I want you as my lover, in all your nakedness," you said.

You move your hand down my legs, as though to brush off a fall of sand and I move under your touch. At such movements, we are lovers and I remember swimming with you, waves around us, wetting stray strands of my hair and wrapping them like strands of dark seaweed around your neck.

I begin to laugh; my shoulder blades, in a movement, change the rocks of my spine. The land belongs to my past. So many thoughts abandoned, there is a pile of stones on the floor. My hips rise slightly as if someone has placed a small pillow in the small of my back. Sometimes I feel you touching me with your hands, and how you hesitate before you move away, as though you have been making love to me with your eyes. It is not a matter of letting something come about passively but of you bearing down on my image.

There is something simple about your images; they are almost like private places you would like kept secret, but have decided to give a hint about what these private places might be. My image filled with falling light. Should you have been concerned at shadows... as if a stray piece of sun was falling into the room.

Lying on the bed watching you work, I see you, as the scene itself, as you stand there, holding the side of the canvas with one hand and with the other, a brush...and I am almost laughing; and I keep moving my lips, as a woman who wants a kiss from you. You can detect how a smile collects itself at the corners of lips and spreads across boundaries of a mouth, a migration like hot lipstick  spreading on water.  I watch you slowly paint a brush line of crimson; the paint pulls softly through sable, spreads out and leaves a moist stain.

Every correlation between two people is given away and found. Yet none are visible to the naked eye. Something breaks through when you touch for the first time. You fall in love outward, as if in the falling, pulse; sweat and blood are similar weight. One moment more, a kiss on a mouth, when you transcribe feelings with lips, the tongue's wet syllables, pressure of your mouth. Soft stabs punctuate text of kiss. One moment more, a night of discovery, close connubial sweat, yet it is just the beginning, I can love you, if you let me. Our bones together in the dream of another life. All I can think about is you.

When you paint my smile, I get an overwhelming feeling that we will lose each other. If I accidentally leave you, wait for me, I will be back. Sometimes you feel like a paper kite, at times I feel you tug away from me, rise up and float out of my grasp. Then I will watch you until I lose sight of you.

Others loved you and have fallen through, discarded when you left, one face pressed against a window of your studio. Wrote you a note on the pane, indecipherable in breath fog, rusted with nostalgia. Other women loved you too much, or not enough. The light changes as light always does. The light casts a grid shape on to the wall of the studio, like a sundial, it casts a slow shadow across the room, it gives no time of day. Looking at you, I am not sure whether it is my own shadow, or whether we are casting shadows over each other. Last shadows stay in enduring form, forever remains of a day.

Something compels you to paint a complete scene with me. The atmosphere is bluer. Is it light stolen from above. From the heavens. Not that it matters one way or another. You paint me with light in my hair; I enter the painting from left to right. Then the paint stops.

You lock the door from the inside. I am a virginal student of love. Yet, I touch your body as if I have touched you before. And then my body suddenly remembers. Sheets crumpled by the unquietness of lovemaking, tossed off in sultry heat until our vibration is music inside me.

Lying in the full light of the sun and by the glare; the weave of the sheet, pores of skin, even my eyelids when I shut my eyes. The artist sees. You transfer the sheet and my body into chromium white, tissue-like images, the rising of my hips, a bridge arching between two pieces of cloth, the residue of movement of your hand as you touch me, the scrim of white.

Days in your studio make me forget my rule. I only intended to stay with you one night, but then the way you kissed me as my head touched the pillow. All our clothes on the floor spread over everything, a white sheet thrown off (a body in perspective).

A young woman enters a man's senses through the pupil of his eye. The sister of nature passes through this tiny entrance, (the measurement of a figure) through a pinprick the vast image of all you see in me, do you sense my cells and moisture; between your eye and me, is this atmosphere I suffuse in you. The artist studies angels, though when you look into my eyes you do not see one. You see the image of a man smiling back. In this way, you occupy a small part of me, but you cannot see the edges of your own lips or any familiar detail of your body. So you do not recognize the man I see, unless the features are defined, you can be any man, seen through my eyes.

Later, you surround me with light and shade, but I carry my own light and shade. Sometimes you sketch me in bad weather or in deep dusk as evening falls, the walls with black and the shadow of the roof eaves fall through the window, across the studio floor. Beyond the wall, the width of summer day's folds into ghost palms, and in this light, the falling of one day into the next, in this slow burnished light, you say my face looks perfect. And the man reflected in my eyes is smiling.

In one significant painting, the light is left as distant as possible, a soft light comes through the un-curtained window, then vanishes. You compose me, legs slightly apart, and the sun paints the skin of my thighs with flickering patches of light. There is magma warmth; you follow the gradual shadows cast between my thighs until it is lost in a darker shadow. My hips bury themselves in the folds of fabric. And then, gently rise out of them. You sense night and morning mingled with my honey. The color of my savannah, marked by wild grasses and me.

For a while we live in your studio without much money; Sometimes a piece of cooked fish and oysters from the Greek fisherman. You are the generous one. You make me a birthday present of a cardboard box. A bird flies out when I open it. One worn mattress from the bed of a whore. Sleeping on the bones of a skeleton, (some objects possess bony relief). Further than the studio room, into the place of crows, poison red berries ripen slowly in the hedgerows. In wild lovemaking, with no practical purpose, your paintings watch us. But our exposé makes their eyes close. Lust formed by our own bodies, catches between the nakedness, at a thousand boundaries of sex and the last fence-line of sleep, the scent of apple blossom outside the window, the muscle of the moon swelling into evening, the threshing in sheets, one dog barking in the distance.

Things that happen in my life are brought together through you. You and I are closer to life's blood on these nights. The nights we are given to conceive, (boundaries we can no longer define) a kiss, given and taken, perfectly received, and love strengthens with all that is given, the moment is all; fertile nights when our shadows move, the strength of the moment, for thousands of tiny cells render in the heat.

The infant in our arms, beautiful baby blanketed for winter belongs to us and the room, (introducing a great fire) the fire is red dyed deeply into the blood and color black oak burn of night. It is the only color. Between you and me and the fire and our baby in the half-light, the edges of flames light up our skin.

You paint me naked. For the soul, you say, is changed either by the passions of the body or according to its own passions. Painting requires practice, it requires a repertoire of positions that you pose me in. Painting where I stretch across the bed, then lean back so you can draw my face.

"Where do you first begin when you paint a woman?" I ask. "I begin with the eyes, as light, the hips, the folded sheets, the falling light, and I look laterally at what causes an image to smile, the moment before the color of beginnings." I am sure you come close to telling me a greater truth.

At this point, I am standing close, I raise my head and you bend down and kiss long and slowly on my throat... my lips part, a kiss on a mouth, litmus of kiss, this time your tongue pushes into the moist center parting on a mouth. The rest is symmetry. Like the first time you spoke my name. (No). You did not speak. It felt like your voice broke my name, breaking it open, like an ancient seal. My hair appears to be flooded in blue. If this is true, am I the river. The wind. If I change into the colors of things close to you. Will I be rain in your eyes. Wind pulling you back. But this does not happen in this room.

Private images blur to "painterly" effect in your usual manner, on a large scale, it gives you nowhere to hide. Sittings go on for hours, days, sometimes weeks, as I hold a position until, growing tired, my hands and limbs fall into each other. You appear uninfluenced. When my limbs, my breasts are painted with heavy black ink, my hair is falling leaves; your hand feels my heart beating under the bark; and the branches: you hold them as if they are limbs, in the orchard of another garden. The shadow moves behind the shutters - four o'clock and the rain falls on the roof of the room; both words and memory have visual content, moving between life and death and in the waking dreams and worlds we touch.

It is the brushing of one image against another. Your canvas is emptied of all but the wound separating flesh and blood.

Why does an artist draw? "Life is never without a scar," you said. "So you will draw my features true to life. The tiny scar under my lip?" I ask. "A body reveals scars, as if by accident," you said.

In the semi dark rooms we read each other naked. A haze of blood, a piece of pain. Each cut each bruise, you never heal. I want to discover the origins of you.

"I paint you in my heart, imprinted, and with such pressure, that nothing can erase the deep embossing unless I rub my own heart out," you said.

"When I see something beautiful - a throat, a belly – my hand wants to paint it. The desire to make an image – I seize the woman as the object of imagination. It has always been this way."

I was not present in the moment when you entered your art, but each time you paint your face becomes more handsome. Even as the years pass. It is a creative phenomenon. As if there is an altitude you reach, in a place far above you, that renews you.

When looking at you working, I become aware of the rigid structure underlying the surface. All the portraits in the series are the same, with both arms open and with the open mouth facing either left of right. Line and pattern, allude to something deeper - to the interconnectedness of all things. The witness. I saw you bleed. I see all your brushstrokes. They are about one woman. The one in your studio. The one in your bed. I am the only one you configure love for. I take the seed and the glistening core of you. The shrine of all bones and what is in my soul. The real one. I am against the night. The dark side of me gives your work tension no one else can understand.

Your body is answered by mine. You let go your breath in a sudden rush. As if you have been holding your breath for a thousand years. I see your floating heart.

White canvas is silence. I hear the echo of white, the shadow of lead behind the paint, when inspiration comes to meet you; it comes from a land beyond the bone. "I understand white," you said, "I've seen dreams crumble, snap and break like well-preserved wishbones. Been blinded by rice grains drying in oriental sun. The frozen blindness of white as powder snow. The white of nautilus shells, eggshells, and crushed pearls. There is bone white, burned gritty and gray. The white of haze of ghost."

"I prefer to make my own white paint from the stones," you said, pointing to white stones in cardboard carton. Stones as large as a fist, others the size of a baby's fingernail. "Where do they come from?" I ask. "So much in life comes from the sea carried by oceans," you said. I watched you rub until the stones became rich and oily. Completely smooth. But you leave your canvas unpainted.

You understand white but what about color? "Can only an artist find pure colors?" I ask.

"Color is an obsession. Last night, I dreamed I was surrounded by powdered pigments of every hue. I picked them up before they slipped out of my hand. The five pigments for your skin, the crimson for your lips, the powder in a bowl was already brightly stained, blue azurite for your eyes, and black made from charcoal to draw the outlines of your curves. All flowed out. I painted you. I opened the paint box and painted until I ran out of color." "What do you do when color runs out, what then?" I ask.

In the foreground, Oriental embroidered birds and peach trees. When I slip my arms through a sheath of silk sleeve. I feel like perfume spills over me. In my heart's mind, there is no abacus to count these moments. But it isn't just about days of modeling for you. I am left with images of interwoven things in the time I spend with you. An image of your dark hair on the pillow falling over your eyes as you turn your head to look at me, that slow turn of your face, as your mouth opens and whispers to me, as if your body shares the secret of its stones. You share them with me.

Just as I refine my thoughts towards you, your thoughts break into facets. The sketches in the black journals. They remind me of us. Expressions of desire, strong uninhibited lines. Your paintings are deep in symbolism and metaphor.

When ink is applied to paper, paper reacts, attracting and absorbing to create images that are partly your own intention and partly due to the paper's own sensitivity.

In your paintings I see the living woman whose power, the air, earth and sea resembles. I see color, as late afternoon, the sun catching fire as sunset turns the world to gold. I see you paint me as perfume, exotic aromas and eastern sandalwood on the wall. Painted in white, I set wet silk on fire.

You paint me as someone who can speak to the plants, stars and earth, the cache of words determining fate, curing sickness, and aloneness, stirring vital passion, the arousal and seduction of all men. Your woman, pure line and light precisely rendered a testament to designations of the feminine elements.

And then there are a series of mutual images, neither lost nor hidden in their sexuality, a brush weighted with ink. The earth of women you temporarily inhabit. There are messages from you written into the paintings. Like a string of time. I see messages and meanings hidden for me to find. It feels like a list of instructions for discovering the Divine. There is Venus you sculpture for me, small enough to fit in the palm of my hand. And her face stares at me and her lips go on speaking. Few people hear this.

Abstract images with Venus inscriptions of the female body. Worn as pendants, placed in graves, and sculptured from polished clay and mammoth ivory. Rendered part bird, part snake, holding a crescent moon, a child, or phallus, these earliest representations of the female nude linger in collective pre-consciousness. One woman educates the other in the nature of love: physiology, sexual techniques and the differing psychology of man and woman, various degrees of physical beauty. She is symbolic of something we have.

"You and I are created for making love," you said, "and when we begin to love we begin to live and everything we do is focused around feelings for each other. So you'll continue to pose nude for me?" you ask. "Many times. Because you look. Perhaps I am obsessed by it. I think you are too," I said.

I open my drawers. Revealing my flowers of perfection, at once silken underwear, soft briefs, and all women's intimates, sanctified by delicate perfume. Flowers of every color, lacy and embroidered. From violet to fuchsia, petals from every shade of damask rose to oriental orchid, from satin reds to tulip blacks, from hyacinth blues to gardenia white. The entire topiary of female concupiscence. "They are my privacy. They are my documents. You can have one," I said. You touch the inventory of sexuality, smooth one out with care and write my name and yours on the silky surface, fold it briefly and put it in your pocket. Is an artist a voyeur? I wonder.

The relationship of an artist looking at his model naked is one which allows the viewer to see truth of their existence of desires in art, or, through art, as a physical body emanates desires. Do you use voyeurism, the act of one person looking at another, to draw us to the source of desire? The way of all flesh where nudes seduce the eye. Yet, your most erotic picture does not have a body in it, unless you count the slightly parted halves as a body. The sexuality of vision. What is revealed?

There is this much-used prostitute's bed, with its worn out mattress. It holds the bodies of each clandestine act. But only the ecstasy from you lover, will I remember after many years. I shall not forget these divine portals of love or the paintings created; paint grayness through cigarette smoke; paint clarity through ice in a glass, the way you paint me. Until in every painting, the brush remembers me. You touch my shadow and I stay... to slide down your canvas.

Still, I know, I am not the first woman you painted. As I detect the taste of wine on your tongue, I know I count for the smallest grain of balance. "Once I found a letter under the bed. She said she loved you, is it true?" I ask. "I merely drew her," you answer. Naked drawing of a woman on the wall in your studio. That was it. So why do you keep the drawing of the woman. For what?

Suddenly I start to translate the drawing into poems. I am held by a gust of thought, and I cover your drawing in words. Did you take out a small red book from your pocket and sketch her too? Did you call her beautiful and celebrate. And by the end of the night, is it what she loved: the mixed-up smell of your bed, intimate spaces of double things. This room, this bed, this mattress? Nothing fits, nothing planned, everything disarranged.

I look around your studio and see nothing

is new. Bought from flea markets. Everything here is used. A single wardrobe and a chair covered with faded blue velvet, with memories of mingled scent of musk, oil and damp hair. I do not know whose hands touched you before mine. What lists of tricks, flirtations mastered, lists of what a woman learns to do: if your hands explored her shape or you touched her with the heat of your fingertips. The alchemy of your body, what metallurgy happened. Sound of rusted bedsprings trapped in some sweet ambush.

These thoughts burn with intensity as if someone opens the door and releases a thousand fireflies in the darkened room. When does a man become a woman's possession? When does a woman become a man's possession? Do I use you like a habit when you hold me? And what does it matter. Habits of sex reveal who I am, the phenomena of life concerned with sexual desire, informal sexual gratification. The women you knew before me have disappeared from your mind. Now do you keep them, secretly, behind your smile.

In this astrology of sex, you touch me. I find unbelievable contrasts, being a young girl, yesterday's innocence and now as a woman, the sound of the dress as it slips off my shoulder. The light is low in the sky and as dusk falls, it fills the room with tangerine light that traces a perfect shadow of the ghost palm on the inner wall. Touch me. Hot sun, cool fire tempers with seductive words, black shade, shine sun, burn fire. A woman in the field of Venus.

Ha Noi. This city lies within a river bend. Its name means a bend in the river. But in some confusion, the city has had at least seven names and sometimes the boundaries moved.

There is an ancient pagoda. When they rebuilt it in the 15th century, in the foundations of stone, they found a statue of a woman. She was then worshipped in the pagoda. Two hundred years later, the walls need rebuilding. Each time they were rebuilt, the walls collapsed. So the men dug the foundations deeper and each time they did, another statue of a woman was found. It is said that when all the women are unearthed, the walls will hold fast.

This was a place of rules: climb down from your horse. Walk on foot. Carry the corpse of the past over your shoulder. Two thousand years of time, it knows the way. The path leads to a second courtyard. A gate left open should be closed.

North of the old city is White Silk Lake, which once had a palace with a hundred roofs. It is reached by a narrow lane lined with stalls, women selling breadfruit, roses, paper votives; giant snails and fried fermented shrimp cakes.

The museum is down this street, thousands of rusted arrowheads and three bronze ploughshares. I do not claim the barracks of bloody histories. On the walls assassins fans, unhinged they flutter and lock and kill; a structure of death wings. Black Chinese ink.

Ink and brush move, upwards and downwards and between, as if a hand moves to touch, lifting veils where masculine and feminine elements are in harmony.

I hold a tiny magnet engraved with poetry, and I see first things…what I imagine… I see you across arcs of moon, I see you fall through the stars. An uncontrolled fall beyond the usual hold you have on yourself.

You are such exquisite hell. Lethal addiction. You take the night and frame it for sex, maybe a little atonement. Sleep-walking into years, your eyes are fluent as though nothing else matters. "Why do you like women?" I ask. "As honey," you said.

And then you fall back to sleep, my pillow pressed lightly against your cheek, your face, beautiful. Held to the passions of the body, I am beautifully adulterated, by you. Like a thick pulse that has not been broken, it has always been that way. Yet I can see echoes of a face seen in the past by other lovers. How her kisses might have touched your face. The first vision of her in an angel's mask.

I look in your eyes. I am no thought-catcher, but I guess you are sad. Love strikes in a thousand shivers, and break us without warning.

Images return. Trail through doorways of my mind. Appear and disappear; images transfer among fish and ink and white sheets crumpled by this biology, this intimate theology. Our room as a cave at night, a tent in sunlight, a Baroque pavilion late afternoon. The sexual shadows, friction and passion. Then your body arches in the curtains ravine. Red silk. Looking at you, the moment's surrender, softly denude of shadow.

I came on my own and have been sleeping there under your earth. Room by room. Touch by touch. Midnight sex is real. I can hardly stop myself. For we are like torches of wax. One thing is shaped by the other.

In a white painted room full of titanium crystals, so many of them airborne, they drift from the white painted walls on to my body and land on my skin as your paintings fill this room. A hundred strokes you paint and then stop and start again. In the painting, I wear a white silk slip with nothing underneath. But the material is only thin as cloth is, so you can see through the fabric, the triangle of black delta; the half-opened thighs spread and give way to your lines.

I show you things you do not know. I reveal orgasmic secrets without markers, enclosed secrets and exposed secrets to you during the night. Your mouth on my mouth makes the earth moan. The magma in the spine and all bones melt, deep laid nerves like secret maps for deep laid routes into my body, the revered anatomy of this bone, and how it fuses inside, is pilot-less. Our hearts are arrowed with loss, even before we met.

I lie my head on your heart, a heart beating with its river, deep within your side. It is wounded by love. I hear it bleed. I say nothing, for nothing is left to be said. I engraved you on my heart years ago. I daydream small fragments and if you could move my thoughts like the grasses or pull them apart like the wings of a butterfly, one by one, you will find a story attached to each.

Did we met by chance? You say nothing in the world happens by chance. Chance becomes the spaces between the shifting arrows of time. The arrow moves towards a fixed point and is nothing but an impulse received from the archer. Whatever is natural reaches its end by its own accord. This endless genesis.

We drink wine and talk about scraps of things in gypsy words... pieces of gold, doves/ sheets, moon/ a thief/those who steal at dusk and daylight, guns/candles. You (smile) how good it is to make conversation...commandments/ saints /to rob a person asleep, lanterns/eyes, a spy, and dancing/to take flight...to go.

The baptism of thought, the thought bless-ed, by their sound the birds frighten and depart and the winds and words scatter us.

If you could see our house, our door opens. A bed, a desk. And in the realm of a house, my papers are folded like a flock of birds, from room to room. As many birds in cages and white peacocks on green lawn. Until a woman at the market said kill all your birds, except birds with white feathers, like the paper you write on, no other explanation.

Of all our assassinations which are natural for us, you say, it is done with the hand, by converting fingers into tongues, words unspoken are entered, as the birds' ethereal flight after silver knife cut a throat, as many words as the transcriber writes so many wounds the birds receive. A flock may be saved by the calligraphers, transcribers and illuminators of manuscripts.

"Poet, you are born with a mouthful of birds. The doves against the new moon. It is to bring back the birds; to re-enter your text. Write about what you know. Write about us. This love I feel for you. Write of the look you give me with your emerald eyes. If Dante could see you now, he would speak of your eyes as emeralds: Purgatorio, xxxi. I note you have no necklace, nothing but bare skin at your throat. If Lami could see you know he would write of you in his Annotazioni, Erano I suoi occhi d'un turchino verdiccio, simile a quel del mare," you said. We talk about scraps of things in gypsy words...until the touch of your lips is felt even after you leave. I love you; your eyes are the same color green as mine, to speak ay ojuelos verdes with the one who catches my smile, leaves me with a desire for you to touch me.

We close our eyes and point to places on the map. We journey together. I am aware of the heat of you, the rhythm of the train as we travel. You press against me in slow motion. On both sides of the track rows of sunflowers appear as far as the eye can see; those yellow petals which betray summer. I stare at the flowers as if I have never seen sunflowers before, imagining the symmetry and whirling pattern of seed. The yellow discs like drying suns and a flight of pink feathered birds (wild pigeon), as they land amongst the flowers.

Then the train pulls out of another station. The train moves on two rails bent by force into a curve, the direction of the line, which it desires to return. There is the rocking of the train, the dark tunnel, the long hard whistle of the train as the long train pulls through. I look off into the fields. They are yellow in the sunset. The sun sets in blood red clouds. I want to hold you. I want to say things to you now that are never said.

Once a season, the farmers have a ritual. They burn old flowers in the fields, in a bonfire; whatever is not alive, they burn. I look out of the apocalypse of burning sunflowers, the sky on fire, and then I look into your face. I feel like we are on the other side. A metamorphous waits.

I read your code so I can find you through all time, when the sun has set, when the moon has set, and the last human fire has gone out, I will find you like a shadow under my heart.

What holds me at gunpoint? How fragile the celebrations are. After days and nights of being with you, we become our own dreams, weightless and rare. With you I travel the world, from city to city.

All things are imperfect, impermanent and incomplete. It's a question of how much we need. There have been times; I never asked what you want from me. I know what you see in me by the way I make you look. All alchemy blends into this.

One winter, we rent a house in the mountains. The windows shuttered and latticed, creating shadows on the snow. I like the atmosphere, the rooms of dusty medicinal almanacs and history books. I like the fractured glass from two bullet holes. And the street light cocooned in fog. We watch snow falling over the streets. The emotion of whiteness, the silence of it. The altitude high, the air white and cold, almost blue. The fire burns as whole storms are left outside.

And here the ghost palm shadows move along the paper, the dark ink running across the page, I see beyond the inky river. And in the background, darkness and shadows of the interior. It is continuous shadow. From closer in, a shiver in your body is answered by me. I see your floating heart. The witness. I have seen you bleed.

We only have ourselves to give. In the arms of a lover, made real by the act of love. Desire for the desire. I love, for my love is made real in the act of loving you. And after, like ghosts and saints, our own voices move like lanterns through the room.

Let me borrow your pencil, I will draw and you will see. The lead breaks. You push too hard. Think of the weight of black on a floating piece of paper, or a strand of hair as a soft line along a neck. A line is not difficult but it has a fate unless you let it float. But the motion takes place without you forcing it. You can't fake it. You cannot draw if your hand does not follow your eye. Your hand must not follow your mind. Your eye and soul must draw together.

"I would rather make love to you than draw

on this paper. But how have I done here?"

You draw roses and kisses with prayers and promises. Vows irrevocable. The ones that slip out of your mouth. I hold your body to it. Velvet is on your bones. It rubs off on mine.

The only pattern I can conceive is you. Like a sleeper you turn in my dream, and as you move, you move the sheet before you. I watch your hands open the fingers of the angel nailed to the clouds. You turn the Angel's feathers into ivory with your brush, almost, but not quite, you make her cry. And the sound comes to me: the first sound of loss. I am wondering if you hear it. First the loss of a bird. Then the loss of a cat. As if all tiny losses add up to the final loss. Prepare me for leaving you. Or you for leaving me.

An artist is given to stare, his brush balances between the index finger and thumb of his right hand. Undressing before the mirror, where you can see me, I let everything fall way, fall to the floor. You paint the sweep of flesh. Uncovering and covering in the middle of nowhere, who cares and for all the night passions in your room, what you kiss and what I kiss for you, and by the time morning light enters the room, with all the heat and marrow, the middle is sweeter, when your eyes open. I look into your eyes. I want to tell your beautiful face to hide from growing older. Sometimes, I think you know my words before I speak them.

You listen to breathing through the white; see my eyes close, for I am the only sleeper in your white canvas, framing the woman, looking at light and shadows some primitive cosmology of caves, deep chasms and earths own fire; the sheets glistening with juice and seed.

In the biology of the blood, I am like every woman. I have been there forever and I have never existed. The body is the way it is, this love I have always had, from the beginning and before when I loved you in all your moments. You and I lay as the sands lay, and move as the days move, one moves slowly into another. A body's course.

As we sleep listening to the sound waves make. Sleep shuts our eyes, now no more eyes but shining stars, crystallites reassembling water, which is always the same color as it runs.

The day turns yellow, sand catches between our toes, the sun turns our legs golden – each surface takes on the color of whatever is set against it, you in yellow light, tinged with sun. For memory reworks the interludes of my mind. The sun visible in the sky and we look up to see it; and an artist sees the sun above the sand and the sun sees us from above, for the sun looks down on us as we look up; the sun reflects in one way and but you see it in a day of yellow.

How much nakedness do I have left to give me? We have spent so many days and nights together. How long will I undress for you. Unhooked and folded.

I am lying on a thin sleeping mat made from fingers of bamboo interlocked together. You share the same mat. And in the true intimacy of us – sleeping on dirt floor; the simple places save us; as the grain of dirt survives if it becomes a star. Midnight and time spins away, squeezed past shadows. Tonight the feelings for you pile up inside me. You are author of how I feel. To hold and maintain this delicate point of balance.

I feel the brush as it traces the rocks of my spine. Images are like sand between my fingers… you and I on a blanket spread on the earth. A moon-filled night and all the blue penguins drift out of the mercurial blackness into the breakers. Eyes open to eventuality, to dreams and places. We fall unconscious and at the edge of this world, then gently pull each other ashore. The sun always rising above the ocean, black tui among the red flame trees. Take seeds of flame tree…take manuka flower…the leaf of kowhai… the sound of bird and waves on the horizon, the cold and the old, the stillness of death. Fragments are separated. Fragmentary form, a manner of spacing. Of the known and the unknown.

These moments accumulate and form patterns and I accept you as a sign of destiny. In a way, we hold each other hostage; how many nights we spend together. My desire to make unending love to you with my lips, my hands, my eyes, with all my body as long as I continue to breathe. I love making love to you. I am consumed in the very act of it. What does desire translate to? All desire is desirable. Whispering to me: all desire is translatable.

You paint close up. Your brush moves on the canvas; cambium white air; it begins to accumulate on my breasts and throat. I am wearing a greenstone carving on a plaited string I tied in a knot; the closures so light, it seems that only your fingers can disturb them.

I appear on the verge of abstract, my arm bends forming a blade like image, like a sword, as a woman defending my position. My shoulder blades protrude upwards, creating a horizon. In this reactive pose, my mysteries and beliefs are revealed in the lines of my palm but you do not see this. There is a profound sense of secrecy, as if I can see into the future, but I will not reveal destiny to you unless you ask me.

The door is opened; or the door opens itself. You are compelled to look through the door again and see what is suddenly seen. The power of prediction occurs in moments. If you go before me, leave the door open with your shoe.

There is no weight in words, and the future holds the same light, as if I am writing with water. The weather days rehearsed, the way rain stings my eyes and yet the drops are not salted. And I cannot tell where the rain starts and my tears end the moment before. Fragments of raw glass and threads of flattened gold, I feel you tying them on a string around my neck. "What is it for?" I ask. "For holding sadness," you said.

You tell me you love me as if you would die tomorrow. I draw in a deep breath and trace an invisible route on your palm. Because, you know, when you sleep you are not sure to wake, and if you wake up, you are not sure to lie down again. It is like crossing any border, you take only what you need and leave behind the person you thought you were; you keep moving forward without looking back. There are obstacles to love and destiny. Some are decorated with broken hearts. But they are not our misfortune.

It is clear that you understand profoundly the nuances and tenets of Impressionism, Cubism and Expressionism. But you also understand the intrinsic power of the brush. The relationship of the ink to line to black to white. Energy, positive and negative. You tell me that to create something new, one must not have a past. The shadow of my spine unhinges the image. The finished painting, when exposed to light, over time will fade. "How will you remember me?" I ask.

"In water," you said, "I like to think of you, standing in the shower. I know all intricacies of where the water goes." Then your smile, watching me, as I am watching you. A cross-current of earlier love, a hundred fathoms deep. "We are water," you said.

If they ever ask me for an identifying mark, I will tell them it is just a bluish bruise of fish in circle. I will tell them: you can swim, you have always swum.

I find in dreams a place of wind and wild flowers and seaweed, rock crevices full of pearly shrimps brought back from this Pacifica world where color, like love, like life, is nonreturnable. There are degrees of existence, like degrees of heat and chill. And lovers do not exist without the effect of heat on each other.

I wake before you open your eyes. I look at your face, your dark hair, skin seasoned by saltwater and time, tanned where the sun touched you and you wake as if I am waking myself, feel your pulse pulling inside me. Sometimes I wake up and thoughts rise like a river and flood my heart. I wonder, in those moments, do you keep me from drowning.

I see us as dreamers, how things appear to be in a moment, behind and beyond. The sun shining yellow neon after the rain. I am dreaming and forgetting. Of transparency of fish slipping in fresh blue waves. Waves breaking backwards, and fishing canoes coming home. Some beautifully assembled thoughts I discover. Some secret seduction in the waters of the ocean, when you carried me from the ocean to the sand, where you dried me with your body.

It is easy, sitting here in the sand at low tide, deciphering chips of missing rocks and broken stones, curved comb interweaving sea kelp's damp darkened hair. Unraveled in the riddle of king tides, crippled blue stingers littering lip of shore. Serpentine jelly ribbons, flowing like poisonous rivers crisscrossing the sand.

When we kiss, I taste salt that has been carried on our skin, like pollen from infinite oceans, the ways of the sea and us. A frieze of seascape. You open the basket and I look inside; the translucence of tua-tua are white glitter; the water-silk iridescence of paua shells, gathered up in a flax basket. We fill a bucket with seawater and you put them in deep soak. They spit sand at night.

Our needs are simple. There are many days when we gather shellfish at the rocky inlet near the headland. Some shellfish forbidden. The green-tipped mussels. We stay in the foam, only long enough to take them.

You teach me how to shake rules from my blood. You show me the old world, nomad, gypsy, raider, sailor; to live without apologies. To be a woman at the place of rocks. How the beach is our survival; it gives us food and the warm sun that will not wear out. A place we find that shines and burnishes us, and unlike the city, does not tarnish us. That is how the days go by.

At the beach we loosen the mouth of the net. We each catch similar fish. Seeing you smile holding fish against a backdrop of blue Pacific Ocean, a photograph of us as we kiss. A pencil drawing you make for me, of me, as I lie in the sun. The sun thins lines of trees and casts sundial shadow over my eyes. In the background, a section of faded driftwood fence, the remainder stretching from dunes to the foreshore, rusted wire tangled.

Above us, a thin blue strand of dragonflies. Their cellophane wings beating in a line above the rocks. Crimson pohutukawa pregnant with blossom. Ruling the evening, a ruby sun sets in the flat sea.

Before the city, before buildings were arranged – we stayed closer to the sea. These islands of Aotearoa, covered in a long primal cloud, cutting a pause in the sacred bush. Between these two islands…as if thoughts are inlay, or overlay … there are deep channels cut by a sacred hand, a handclasp dissolving and reforming, the great hand dividing land that joined Aotearoa together. You found me sleeping in a room laden with birds of paradise in the fabric: Pacifica of lime geckos fighting on the ledge of ginger leaf, bush of kowhai and manuka trees, green moss and silver fern. Native bush of wet dark velvet outside the door, with the odor of green resin. When I left the window open, the sound further into the room, of surf pulls towards us... puckering up over sand, then throws back as deep sound-boom.

I follow your footprints, only to discover them disappearing and reappearing. Sometimes into the surf. I continue to follow footprints until I make out a familiar shape, sitting in the same place were we always sit. You watch me approach, with a smile on your face, a carbon pencil in one hand, closer up, I can see that you have drawn me in a series of kinetic shapes, as you watching me coming. A thin dog following my heels. You finish the drawing and write the date.

You have a different way of looking. Sometimes it unnerves me. I don't know how to explain. But your eyes look deeper into what you desire and take possession of it. That look of seeing. As if you see more of me and in this consciousness: I make me appear. And yet, you take me by surprise.

"I see you, I know you and I want you," you said, " each line is physical. If I see you, you will not become lost to me."

I know life should be as simple as foot-prints. I follow your wet footprints, the prints of each step, each time your foot moves. Somewhere between waking and sleeping, I think of these moments, the way I know blue feels in mornings, as water, and the sun stirs us, like a bed of em-bers, an unending ribbon of heat. The waves of phosphorescence and lucid lines of sand for lov-ers to find in the morning. A door opens. You see me in a towel, my hair up. I close the door, reach up and put my arms around your neck.

Lovers live in the palaces of each other, map within a map, tent within a tent; like the nomads, the wanderers, pilgrims of the trackless road. Grass etches your feet. Rain drumming on the earth. There are seeds cast before us, sweet incantations sprouting, no longer the uncon-scious traveler trampling into dust, now they car-ry the harvest of us. Living wild without regret. This Divine exile.

"So you came back," you said.

"I hardly moved from you," I said.

Your river runs through my veins. Wild birds still follow the canoe. We never left each other. That is the truth as I know it. Sounds of us come back to us. I turn and look at you. I am holding out my wrists to you and you to me with imaginary rope. These are the emissaries of remembered things.

We return to summer with the rituals of shaking out the bedding and ceremonies of cracking open scallop shells with a diver's knife. As years pass, our children left the tin bucket and spade in the sand, falling in love until they return just for an afternoon and the secret trail down to the beach is overgrown now with indestructible wild ginger, rusted wallflowers and orange flowering nasturtiums. Overhead the sudden burst of scarlet blossoms falling from the Christ tree like a cloak of fresh blood. The trees catch my eye like fire on the hill.

The sun is hot and yellow. It scorches ribbons of clouds and the blue sky. It's the ghostly shriek of tui; dies and comes back to life; every native bird carries in him the memory of bush that is always damp, the vague stirring of leaves, and the immense brown hand that covers the earth.

We are left alone with the leaves, with all the leaves, fanned out, turn rotten then silver filigree skeletons, they give you a feeling of bare feet where ghosts come and go. Bones, spears, shells, bone hooks, woven baskets with purple kumera. Down to earth, the root and seed in detritus, back up to leaves, how many days did the rain spill over them.

Kick off our shoes. Walking down, you and me both barefoot. We follow the path through its rocks and shells, down to the track to the remote bay with its white horseshoe of sand and blue ocean. I am overwhelmed by the gusts of ocean, the strong salted brine and sharp iodine, wet kelp necklace; if you kiss me, the smell from the sea on my skin, the heady jasmine mingled with amber resin of kauri gum in my hair. I know the loneliest part of the beach, the remote cove, between thick columns of pohutukawa trees anchored in cliffs that are red and yellow with clay.

We swim. The light from the sun filters through the surface. A ribbon of sapphires. Not solid gems but tiny particles crushed as if they were ultramarine blue cerulean ground by a great pestle: Prussian blue to cobalt with tinctures of indigo and shades of lapis, it is like swimming into all the beach glass of civilization sparkling before us. I see the same blue in your eyes. The water holds us like a secret.

"Is what you imagine, more real that what you see?" I ask. You smile. "I see origins of you." You arrange driftwood on to the fire. You pile the salt-bleached logs in a strong structure, leaving deliberate spaces for fire to breathe. You light the fire, using matches you have inside your jacket. And as the fire burns of its own accord, you pick up the blanket and wrap it around us.

The composition on the beach: sand blows through my mind, it catches in our hair, dusts over arms and legs with emery grit - the sand holds the print of a footstep; we take turns stepping into each others marks, touching you with bare feet as if my soul is walking on you, a foot reversing the location of toe and heal; sand is the material in which the print is made, the sandal under Hermes' feet. Yet, these movements are not rehearsed, when I walk with you, from the far end of the beach, your hand holding my hand. A step seen from the back. Some external force seems to know us.

We stand on the same land. The little patch of shrine where we hold each other. What is yours is mine. There is nothing to indicate that our existence has been overlooked or forgotten in this place, the circles of sun and moon render the same illusion, day after night. An aura of the other, like a halo, we are seen together.

If I go some distance away from you, I will be able to recognize who you are because of you. If I go further away I will still recognize you. Further still and distance will still not diminish the way I feel about you. For this law of distance does not apply to the law of desire.

You have changed and yet there is something about you, unchanged. Years grow around us; the rooms and houses look familiar, the cities and countryside, the water, new and ancient.

Memories awake now, the relics of sensation returning, your smile, and your face made hard and everlasting. Then, this thick wet canvas. Black drawing of night. The stanza of jet and silk, its seductive lines slipping off paper, the painting keeps up its quiet breathing, as if breathing is some law of living. That is the mix-up of all loving. It is not perfect. Just human. So we make love, using up our life in a slow way, among our heartbeats. I turn to you. When we are together, I have the feeling of fastening, unhooking returning to the starting point with you.

I go back to the same room, the silhouette of the palm tree and lantern of moonlight. I feel the vertigo too; the immense drop out of the warm bed inside this scant room, a room is not our home, a mattress low on the ground. Sheets still feel hot from our bodies as if they have been kept warm in the belly of the house. The intimacy of us, nocturnal shifting moving bare under the covers. Still, I am comforted by the overlay of you, some identity of our younger selves, like faded blankets,

The intimacy of us, defined by our substance, like water, it has no left or right. Infinite and unlimited. A woman is loved the way it is for the lover.

If I speak of our road, Lover, I shall speak of a time when you are left to count what remains on a few fingers, the lines on the palm of your hands, the fragments of a life that was, patterns, rhythms, riddles and rhymes of us in our time.

I give the past to you, in the hope that it will not fade from exposure; before the negatives develop, the pigments of hurt blurred and forgotten. By giving away past memories, will the burden of the past fall away from us. The sharp apex of pain, marks the extremes of life's fractured plan.

Some paintings show the same dark hearted influence. Until there are parts of you, breath, skin, voices, that feel like a stranger. I realize now, how impermanent everything is, how fragile the moments, how changeable, how temporary, how we take familiarity for permanence, but we by nature are the most impermanent.

"What are you doing for the rest of your life? I feel like sleeping through it," you said.

Some people may be disturbed by your voice, and the images you paint, in which the images are trapped.

"You are living the wrong way round," I said. "Put love first. And the rest of life can fall into place. Do that one thing for me?" But what you tell me is this… what we need most now is to figure a way to have a roof and food on the table.

"If you atrophy sensuality and other senses, taste and feel will follow," I said. What we say to each other goes dead, as if the operator cuts the connection. Then I wonder if we have suddenly changed; after our things are broken and scattered, our souls are remembering, waiting in the ruins of it all. In a tiny drop begins the recollections over and over again; how did we get this faraway from each other.

*(Artist's letters to Poet)*

So the summer left. You left and I could capture neither one. I did not want to say good-bye. I wanted to be leaving with you. Terminal is a word for an ending. I felt you inside my body and couldn't leave until you had flown. I couldn't drive out of the car park until the tears had stopped. I waited a long time.

If I could remove the months following your departure, I would take away three months that followed it. The rain. Often in the night room, the rain followed more rain in the diary of grief, each night turning into torrential down-pour, my eyes wet by morning. I was drowning. I ached with this sense of departure. Its scenario implicates me to a tragic script, devised by a sadist somewhere else.

By the unbearable details, it feels like death reversed... it comes curving in, this pain of sadness, uncovered from the despair of all mankind, it comes to me without rehearsal, to fall into a deep well, the pit of earth, its heavy damp contains all the spores and seeds of earths sorrows.

How could I hold the strings of days with you in the warm waves, crumpling themselves against the islands of our naked bodies. Or in the patterns of light cast on your face, under the memory of noon-lantern of mangoes, on the sand that stretched from the headland at Alexander Bay to the grooves of paper-bark trees, their branches traced on the ancient tablet of blue sky? Will these things remain...like the piles of sad bleached bones.

I found the card and a photograph of you

to remind me, as I write this, it has already happened. Like the seeds of the past, folded in a letter, tiny, fertile endearments, sown word for word, made explicit and private, by years of love with you. And I can see you on the beach, held as complex drawings in my mind, which overreach my artist hand. You are so beautiful.

So many memories of you today – for this room is the last place we were together. The tangerine sarong I tied to branches above the tree. It was wide enough for a roof. It turned your body the color of ripe citrus. Now it lays idle across my pillow.

The intensity of found memory only makes me more acutely aware of the love I have for you. Forty-six hours after you left. I'm painting empty. For love, is both visible and invisible, hiding us both. I am the masked artist, by some fated maneuver, both the apostles and Judas as myself.

My moments are filled with you and I have not stopped thinking about you for a single moment. Everything belongs to you, the space of your absence in the bed. Your absence reminds me that I am still here; I miss the weight of you on the other side, scent of you still on my skin. You should have taken these things with you when you left. You are coming and going from me. There is sadness in the coming and going. When I walk back through the door, it is your face I want to see first.

Stood under the outdoor shower in rain, dripping into the grass. Green solitude of the gardens, the variegated leaves the crisscrossing spiders intercepting pathways of sticky juice, the height of the rainforest enclosure. Something moist I remember about collecting liquid in the leaves with you. As if the tropical, the hibiscus flower, the Venus orchid, and giant trumpet flower can devour a man with her nocturnal scent.

When you have limited time, the situation becomes more focused. The sun feels more luxurious, the crickets sing more and the evening air so balmy and then the mosquitoes. The metallic hum of mosquitoes, the living velvet of iridescent butterflies, all of it returns me.

I found my envelopes. I haven't heard from you. I ache when you are sad. You left two incisions. One by a knife which escaped from my hand, the other, this slash of a mouth, a smile, before you told me you were leaving. But it is said, each heart receives a scar.

Marks are a sign that I am alive, proof of human existence. Writing to self, writing alone, telling to a mirror of self, you are my audience in this lonely play and I think survival is in trust, to allow us to find each other again. An astral thread wraps from you to me.

Months apart. I want to kiss you on the mouth and feel your body against mine. I am sick of thinking. I long to splash your green sarong and make it cling to your brown legs. I'm trying to stay in the moment my mind racing ahead of days, weeks till you return. Guessing and desperately trying to find a pattern to move towards you. Without a pattern, the mind lurches like an old wooden cart pulled by a donkey. I am not sure if I am the cart, the donkey or both.

I visited a painter today. He paints scenes of backyards in the city. Gardens without people. Parks of vacancy. I told him it feels like someone is buried there. An ominous presence. His eyes light up. "Yes, yes, don't they!" he said.

I am feeling pressured by the amount of letters winging their way to me. I will write again soon, probably tomorrow. I will get some beautiful envelopes so when you first see them you'll know the letters are from me. In my mind, I am following you around the world. I visualize your every look. One last envelope and the last of the stamps. Monsoon rain tonight I am really missing your person in my life. I feel two-dimensional.

Lately I can't hear what people say, the

sound of ocean in my ears, but what they say does not matter. Only your words. Come back so I can hear the sound of your voice.

I am looking through St Augustine's Con-
fessions, I randomly select passages and browse
through old architectural books, I cut illustrations
of types of vaulted ceilings, tools and systems of
precise measurements, rulers and calipers; then
plot the images and words together, arrive at dif-
ferent permutations, set these on white paper, in
a letter to you, to send man made structure and
thematic psalms from a Saint, who, sees into his
own mind and finds truth in every thought, sug-
gests true essence and eternal qualities, based

on his own understanding of inner nature. The words remind us of still pools, not stagnant, but enriched with the passing of time.

An arch is made up of two parts and each one is weak and wants to fall, one holds the downfall of the other, but together they are converted into a single strength. A supporting beam between two windows. I cannot bear to live as we did before. I want to move away from constant appraisals. From too much consciousness.

Lonely and being alone holds the same weight. I don't want to be alone in the dark. A blanket of dark without the comfort of you. Then thunder and the rains start. We never know which direction we are going, are we entering or leaving. How do we transcend places. Even at distance, the memory of you is tattooed on my skin.

I am falling in love with this place. Pavilion of garden outside the room. Citron trees and oranges and various wild songbirds. Perpetual music and lemon blossom in its weaving. You hear thousands of fig leaves changing color in the tree, the vine on the wall turning bright pink.

The phone rings. You who refuses to be carried away by displacement. "What are you wearing?" you said. You are not as absent as I believed. I am enveloped in nothing. I could never dial this up in an insane moment, but imagine now a voice expressing carnal starvation. I listen to the deep tenure of your voice. The breath of space between. The power to imagine. It restores me to your obsession.

My pathway over the moon as it rises. I come to your bed through lockless doors. To feet barefoot in sand. What is distance but the voyage of us. The weight of water remembers us. "Where do you go when you dream? Do you come back to me?" you ask. "How do you know this isn't a dream?" I said.

Each hour folds like paper in my hands. I piece together thoughts of life. Standing naked in our bare bones, we are older than other human beings, like the rock drawing of the Magdalenian priest, I am struggling with many secrets, that are held as words transmuting private agonies, sweet omens of love, stained with the certainty of death, was something rich and strange, with something universal and personal.

Nights back in my empty room here. I am afraid of empty rooms. Sometimes the roof is filled with sounds of small animals that slip under clay roof tiles above my bed. I sleep, like other women do who sleep alone. Perishable in solitude a woman sleeping alone, falling inwards into herself.

Dense fog, like rain today. There are two donkeys in a field, shrouded in mist; one has a tin cowbell around its neck, both eating low thorny branches. A wild cat under the hedgerow hides for birds. Crickets and grasshoppers chirping. A field of dry grass, cocooned in dewy cobwebs.

You don't see the jewels unless the sun is shining. The shimmer they cast, catches the heart.

Sound of wasps in fig tree. The last summer rose grows against white calcium stones; the climbing rose raises the gray scale in its struggle with the stone wall. When you open the envelope, a hundred petals will fall into your hands. I moisten the closure with my tongue. There is perfume falling into the house. Perfume from a hundred years ago, when the rose was first planted. Now in long sequences it continues climbing.

In this country frame there exists discord between pink roses and the colorless wall, between damask perfume and chicken manure. The sound of hunters' guns in the distance and hum of wild bees. White shutters and blank pages of my journal. Too many mirrors, too many photographs of strangers framed in silver.

I hear the ghost of a shepherd calling his flock. He piles chalk rock on top of rock, he builds a wall through time and four hundred years later

I lean against his structure. There is no erasure, no closure. In the ether of man, your name in the book of time, you exist as Man. In my mind, I am listening to the sound of your voice; I am ready to return to you. Nothing is extinct. It is only us forgetting what is. There are origins in the maze of shadows and fragments, to find your hand leaving its coolness on my forehead. Your face above me. Your eyes looking down into my eyes. The wild part in us. From the pediments of belly. Primitive underbrush.

And so there are the letters, yours and mine, and I open what I know, messages from beyond love's borders. Pilgrims came here by instinct, I was pushed by loss. After the first letter, I can not do anything but think about you, by the time I answer, I see you enter my dreams. I am absent because I am the dreamer. Only you are real.

Letter by letter, your lips are the seal on the back of the envelope. I can detect where your lips lick the glue and your fingers push across the seam. It holds the secrets and protects the opening. Each letter contains late summer. I send roses (when you open the envelope, do not bruise the petals). I will send you winter jasmine, the flowers faintly there.

I recognize Eastern stamps, envelopes often soaked by the rain and secrets asleep in some corner of the envelope. I send miniature verses from Saint Augustine; my mind rests there in the rivers of his book.

Along the road afternoon shadows find the granite stone crosses left for pilgrims walking the different roads of the world.

From the desk in the great room, I send you the circumference of a fig leaf, a feather of a pigeon, the wing of a blue meadow butterfly, yellow petals from tiny chrysanthemums, and French lavender from the bee garden of honey hives. Rain drowns the bees and I steal the honey for my toast.

My long and frequent letters remind me of certain papers we tied to kites with string a long time ago, we called them messengers; some of them the wind used to blow away, others were torn by the string, and a few of them blew up and stuck to the kite.

These letters, my messengers will appear to you like a moments rune or charm, to unriddle surface meanings, then the secondary underpinnings of the words that compose it, and these two patterns are one.

This house is filled with the photographs of immigrants and farmers and peasants, a family in a house. In a black and white photograph, a man who looks like you, he is standing with a woman holding his son. Every picture reminds me of you.

*(The final chapters-Hanoi)*

In the French colonial villa, there is an artist's studio and one large bedroom. In a room of fragrant yellow roses in the Chinese jar, damask perfume dominates the room. The china of many broken dreams tossed at your feet. Anyone who sees you, leaves feeling sadder.

Anyone who comes in sees the suitcases, books and paintings rolled up. There was always a bed unmade and a shirt crumpled in the corner. There is always thought of moving out of the villa, and coming to see me, of going to places never traveled to. It is easy lying there in a room away from the street. Sometimes you can feel the edges of a woman in the room. The sound two gates roughened by distance. Two things close at once.

And all the while, you are moving through this land of poetry and poverty of war. In the city the buildings are broken daily under pick axe and hammer, dust falls inside lungs and on the window ledge of the villa. The air thick with smoke and brick dust. There are other bones, in the archeology of the remaining dream; gateways, mysterious flights of steps falling through the hole in the sky, when all spirits are returning from bones buried at the base of silence.

Vietnamese women selling melons and bread, shelter under blue plastic in the rain. From the back of brick courtyards, the smell of pork belly barbecued over coal fires burning in second-hand ammunition cans. You see dragons run on the apex of the curved tile roof. It is said that the Gods came down from heaven to play with women here. You can smell the woman. She seeps through between the guild and illumination. She has come to cover all the shadows with her perfume. She is inside now. Slowly, oriental colors attract your eyes. And lately, the sound of women's voices, among green rice. You paint on the smooth side of rice paper. They call rice paper, the field of the artist.

There is a desk on one wall, a dresser with woven water lily drawers, shared; clothes I left behind, your clothes closer to the mosaic floor and dust blown in from the street. Sheets on a line strung between the two villas gather paper ash from offerings of burnt money. The noise from the cat on heat, the sledge-hammer of a man working in a nearby room. Around this time, the thunder rolls in after a day of heat. Cracking over the clay tile roof. White lightning flashes in a full light. Rain changes the melon of painted houses. The smell of rain and lime-wash.

The room has high ceilings and tall doors and you keep looking at this, but in this room, your eyes can not adjust to the distance between the floor and the ceiling. The room is not one you painted, the pale yellow walls and green deco ceiling fan.

"I am painting on the shroud of a Jesus, stretched over the bones of my own image," he said to no one. Ghosts form an important part of this oeuvre. When you experience too much, the smell of mould, a rot outside to match the rot on the inside, its dead sensation to sublimate love, a thick darkness of the heart still sticks to memory.

For a while the mind allows the poison to taint what you see, undiluted for this dark air to permeate the structure, until the bones are knitted in black.

When you frame it, you avoid hanging it at eyelevel. Instead you present it on the floor propped up against the wall. Although not obvious, the work feels abandoned.

There is no single way to see everything.

There is just a desire to connect. You look at photographs. In the photograph of the girl reading, she is ignoring the camera eye watching her, the artist standing behind the camera holding her image. The flatness of paper is interrupted only by the suggestive entry of a red book. You keep the photograph next to your bed. Her image is the last image you see before falling asleep.

Some days later, people break into your studio through a skylight and steal the larger artworks. You allow the rain to fall into the studio. At night you watch the stars. The paint is peeling from the weight of thoughts. Some heavy and philosophical, the thoughts come back as if they move in a bicameral rhythm. You spread out all your brushes on the table. Carved handles and red symbols on black painted lacquer. Brush strokes transverse into the air, lines fly into the figurative. As if the soul of you is carried by angels into the gate of the moon. Birds of dreams. The desire of you into me, of me into you.

You paint in black, the definition of your identity and the positioning of your artistic personality in the midst of personal loss. There is nothing left that can be taken. You could hear their human subterfuge making plans underground. Invisible money was bent by others deceits, and treacheries, plunderers of our most private possessions.

You have a preoccupation with aligning, realigning, shifting away from social rules and structure. Options, attitudes, relationships. You depict your own shirt, as if torn from your back. A dark shirt, with a ghostly omnipresence pulling you out as if subjected forever to passing forces.

In your paintings you appear to have made yourself personally responsible for the fate of every human being who views your art.

For you, making studies is not necessary. You paint intuitively and dip into the ocean of us. For those who paint are always in the process of painting. For those who love are always in the process of loving, every moment is a dance. You hold me in the dance of being. The woman you hold and have always held.

It was on the last day of September before the month falls into October, I reach the door of that room lost so far out of the way. I knock on the door. You answer. You are looking at me the way you would look at a traveler. You reach me amongst the dreams... from the debris of your life and my life, already a promise is emerging.

You see my eyes, the level tears rising. I step back into your room as if I never left it. It is a room from another time; you reach out and touch my hair. I am on my way back to your bed...I strip down bare and reveal myself, because I can do it, because I want too.

Let me lie with you, this place is silent and the earth feels warm. Let us stay in the garden and be lovers in the leaves. Such is the connection, in dreams, in daydreams. The memory of the human heart.

Paint me into your own self-portrait, (when you represent me, be honest in what you portray, note that my skin is paler and lines around my eyes are deeper) the faded banks of a smile, the river between, and if you were to ask me about this painting, I will ask you to make another, and another, until you represent us as angels or saints in that time. Or portray us as pilgrims, (but not to many to cause a crowd) as you set us together in the foreground (when we are kneeling down) a larger scale perhaps and then by diminishing the past, make the clouds thinner so the true color of our sky is seen through, where the line of vision sees a road taken (as nothing) disappearing into the distance, make a gate (held by my hand in your hand) and close it behind us, (lock it as you draw it).

Put us back together (arms enfolded) and when I touch you, you hold tight, the way we move into each other. The sad road put behind us. We slowly forgot one winter of loss, when one long season defined remoteness (the blowing of the wind driven and pressed against us) the thickest and densest part of atmosphere lies at ground level and confines life to a delicate boundary (because the thin line passes closest to you), I wept, you heard me, the only way a woman weeps, the way I turned towards you (rope me into your shadow) and as I move, you feel me press down. "You are still beautiful," you said.

Sex, voyeur of this night, you have seen this before. This divine pathway, before I sleep. The scent slipping slowly into my mind and in my thoughts, I know the original outline of you, it is here. I see in your eyes when you wake, a forgotten grain of sleep deep in the corners. These are the emissaries of remembered things.

Late afternoon with you, in this oriental bed lacquered with birds and gold temples, while the women downstairs peel garlic and green shallots. The warm scent floats upwards, painting the air with reds and greens. Then red chili seed and fresh squeezed lime.

Drugged by this afternoon and all nights, I find you here. The mattress has held our shapes as if we have always existed. Everything is just as I remembered it. When I wake, your hands warm under my body.

"Have I changed much?" I ask. You turn your head to look at me. My hair cropped short. My face pale. Paper shadows under my green eyes. This is what you see. "Not at all. Nothing has changed," you said.

We reach out and just lie there. If love is a work of our own composition, it has always remained there, the genesis of us traced back through the rooms and the window frames, and the doorways, after the paintings, after the beaches, and the shoes left at the back door – and if you take steps away from this, the moments remain, after the perfume, after the candles and the linen sheets tangled and twined with the meaning underlying all the sexual artifacts, they are beautiful by their intimate design. Our voices made dents in heaven. This is the grace of remembered things. "You are the only woman I feel whose blood runs through my own veins, as the body of love," you said.

*In this bed we hold together, and when we speak our words drifted on this beach of fallen water. This mended template of our sex, holding us in the physical world, the song of us, the falling of eyelids before sleep. Holding shadows in your fingers, inside the conception, behind the emotion, blind before our eyes returned as the constant river, holding us.*

*Looking back at you through a mask of time, real, existing. And the way you hair falls across my face like soft shadow. Inside my desire and the orgasm, between the sex and the way the binding tightens the drum of my skin. Slow suck of earth and the way you enter me, the seed in the core, the message in the code. The way we exist before we were lovers. For I have known this genesis, to love you was a work of our own com-*

*position. Have known this gold ring and this love affair, we are part of each other; this will explain the first tributaries, like first love running its own course. To match my mouth to your mouth. Your tongue in my mouth, the boundaries diminishing. In this burning. The erotica of memory.*

You look at the last page. The blank one. I have not written there. And so it makes sense to leave the last page blank. It makes the eyes skip the fine print. We cannot leave memory behind, but carry it on our bodies. I felt the quiet sigh, the deep labyrinth of sadness; several angels come back and find us.

You ask me to write a chapter in this book to change what happens to you… I am able to do this, because words are inter-changeable, you can add to them and subtract. You ask me to bring the days back. And this is something I can do. Write us only as lovers swimming in the bay.

You swim about a centimeter from my face, as close as possible without actually kissing; then the waves pushing us closer as into a tight space until sea foam forms a circle stretched around us. Then the taste of salt. You kiss me where the ocean falls  away at the edge of the world. The world  turns red as the sea catches, the sun flames. It burns like fire on water.

Art is found in detachment, in sequestering one vision from a thousand. Love and passion concentrate all existence around one form. If you can paint everything. Why paint anything? Because art, like love, is progressive. We must carry it with us, or we won't find it.

*The heat of summer still continuing, sweat on his body, not wanting to move from under the ceiling fan. Late afternoon and this damp humidity is not the only thing that wakes him. The songbirds in bamboo cage. Someone playing a melodious tune on a fipple flute. Her breathing. A breath of wind. Then no sound but that quiet inlet of water.*

*He looks at her lying beside him, he could paint her but he won't. He doesn't want to change a thing. When he looks again; there is no river, no field, no wind, only a woman sleeping.*

*Pale yellow light slips into the room through blue leafed ghost palms and between wooden slats in the closed shutters. How night turns into another. A personal life deeply lived, expands into truths beyond itself and provides our own answers to the question of a man and a woman's love.*

*About*

# Blanshard & Blanshard

While Blanshard & Blanshard produce their own independent creative works, their deep understanding and respect for each other, enables them to produce collaborative projects together.

Books by Blanshard & Blanshard *'Memoir of Love and Art, Honey In The Blood.'* *'Make Love Last (forever and a day) Fly Me To The Moon And Back'* and *'Make Love Last (forever and a day) Dance Me To The Stars'*.

# BOOKS BY
## *Blanshard & Blanshard*

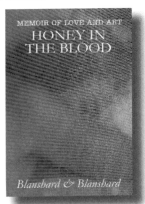

Relationship books. International Bestselling. Available
www.amazon.com   www.pageaddie.net

Susan Blanshard was born in Hampshire, England. She is a bestselling author and internationally acclaimed Poet and Essayist.

Her literary works are published in international journals and anthologies. Selected poetry from *Evidence of Obsession*'and *Perfume River* are published in The World's Literary Magazine, Projected Letters, Six Bricks Press and Arabesque Magazine. Her essays published in Lotus International Women's Magazine, ICORN International Cities of Refuge. PEN International Women Writers' Magazine. PEN International Writers Committee The Fourth Anthology, Our Voice, Biblioteca De Textos Universitarios, Argentina. *The Pillow Book, Four Recipes, The Traveler, Orientation,* published in Arts And Culture, Lotus International Magazine. Collected poems *Running The Deserts, Midnight Mojave* are included in Anthology for the London Olympic Games. Her essay, *Midnight in the Garden of the Temple of Literature* (with Vietnamese translation) features in The Anthology of The First Asian Pacific Poetry Festival, 20012. She is bestselling author of 25 books. Her books of prose include *'Sheetstone: Memoir for a Lover' 'Fragments of the Human Heart'. 'Sleeping with the Artist'. 'Memoir of Love and Art: Honey in the Blood'.*

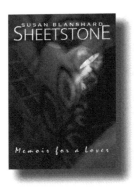 

Bruce Blanshard is of French descent. A bestselling Author and Painter. He has a background as an award-winning Advertising Executive Creative Director. He is the author of 18 books: including *'Naked Hanoi'* a chronology of paintings from the seven years in his Hanoi studios.

Made in the USA
Monee, IL
29 September 2021